EXPLORING
—OUR SEVEN—
CONTINENTS

Australia

HEATHER C. HUDAK

www.av2books.com

AV[2] provides enriched content that supplements and complements this book. Weigl's AV[2] books strive to create inspired learning and engage young minds in a total learning experience.

Your AV[2] Media Enhanced books come alive with...

Audio
Listen to sections of the book read aloud.

Key Words
Study vocabulary, and complete a matching word activity.

Go to **www.av2books.com**, and enter this book's unique code.

BOOK CODE

A 2 4 4 6 7 8

AV[2] by Weigl brings you media enhanced books that support active learning.

Download the AV[2] catalog at **www.av2books.com/catalog**

Video
Watch informative video clips.

Quizzes
Test your knowledge.

Embedded Weblinks
Gain additional information for research.

Slide Show
View images and captions, and prepare a presentation.

Try This!
Complete activities and hands-on experiments.

... and much, much more!

AV[2] Online Navigation on page 24

Published by AV[2] by Weigl
350 5th Avenue, 59th Floor
New York, NY 10118
Website: www.av2books.com

Library of Congress Cataloging-in-Publication Data

Names: Hudak, Heather C., 1975- author.
Title: Australia / Heather C. Hudak.
Description: New York, NY : AV2 by Weigl, [2018] | Series: Exploring our
   seven continents | Includes index.
Identifiers: LCCN 2016051934 (print) | LCCN 2016052251 (ebook) | ISBN
   9781489657435 (hard cover : alk. paper) | ISBN 9781489657442 (soft cover :
   alk. paper) | ISBN 9781489657459 (Multi-user ebk.)
Subjects: LCSH: Australia—Juvenile literature.
Classification: LCC DU96 .H83 2018 (print) | LCC DU96 (ebook) | DDC 994—dc23
LC record available at https://lccn.loc.gov/2016051934

072017
020117

Project Coordinator Heather Kissock
Designer Nick Newton

Photo Credits
Every reasonable effort has been made to trace ownership and to obtain permission to reprint copyright material. The publishers would be pleased to have any errors or omissions brought to their attention so that they may be corrected in subsequent printings.

Weigl acknowledges Getty Images and Alamy as its primary image suppliers for this title.

EXPLORING —OUR SEVEN— CONTINENTS

Australia

CONTENTS

Introduction

Australia is unique among continents, with animals and plants that cannot be found anywhere else in the world. These living things developed distinct features because Australia is an island continent, not connected to any other landmass. The world's largest variety of **marsupials** is found on mainland Australia, which makes up most of the continent.

Several islands near mainland Australia are also part of the continent. The largest of these islands is Tasmania, located off mainland Australia's southeastern coast. Tasmania is separated from the mainland by a 150-mile (240-kilometer) wide waterway called the Bass Strait. Tasmania is home to distinctive creatures, including the Tasmanian devil. This marsupial hunts animals that would otherwise destroy many of the island's plants.

The coastal waters of Australia feature colorful **corals** and fish. The Great Barrier Reef lies off the continent's northeastern coast. Made up of thousands of smaller reefs, the Great Barrier Reef is the world's largest coral reef system. It is big enough to be seen by astronauts traveling in space.

About 6,000 types of sea creatures live in the Great Barrier Reef.

The Tasmanian devil is the world's **largest carnivorous,** or meat-eating, **marsupial.**

Evonne Goolagong Cawley, ranked the world's number-one women's tennis player in 1976, now helps children compete in sports.

Vegemite, a traditional Australian food, is a thick, dark sandwich spread made from flavored yeast.

Deserts and dry grasslands cover a vast inland area of Australia that is known as the outback. Snow-capped mountains are found in other parts of the continent. Few people live in these remote areas. Most Australians live along the continent's southeastern coast, which receives more rainfall than other regions.

Australia is nicknamed the "land down under" because the entire landmass is located south of the **equator**. This continent is known for its moderate climate, as well as for being the driest inhabited continent on Earth. The weather conditions do not change greatly from one season to the next.

Australia's population is diverse. Aboriginal Australians, the first people to reach the continent, arrived by boat thousands of years ago. They built communities in all parts of the land. Europeans began settling in Australia in the late 1700s. They established the nation of Australia, the continent's only country. More recently, large numbers of people from various Asian nations have made Australia their home.

Many artists, performers, and sports figures known around the world are from Australia. Actors include Academy Award winner Cate Blanchett. One of the world's greatest opera singers, Joan Sutherland, was from Australia. Sports stars include tennis champions Samantha Stosur, Rod Laver, and Evonne Goolagong Cawley.

The koala is a plant-eating marsupial that is native to Australia, where it lives in trees.

Australia

The continent of Australia is southeast of Asia. The Asian island nations of Indonesia and Papua New Guinea are the countries closest to Australia. The Timor Sea, Arafura Sea, and Coral Sea border Australia's northern coasts. The Torres Strait connects the Arafura and Coral Seas. The Indian Ocean borders Australia on the west and south. The Pacific Ocean creates the continent's eastern border. New Zealand lies 990 miles (1,595 km) southeast of Australia.

The country of Australia is divided into six states. These states are New South Wales, Queensland, South Australia, Tasmania, Victoria, and Western Australia. Australia also has two territories, the Australian Capital Territory (ACT) and Northern Territory. Canberra, the capital city of Australia, is located in the ACT.

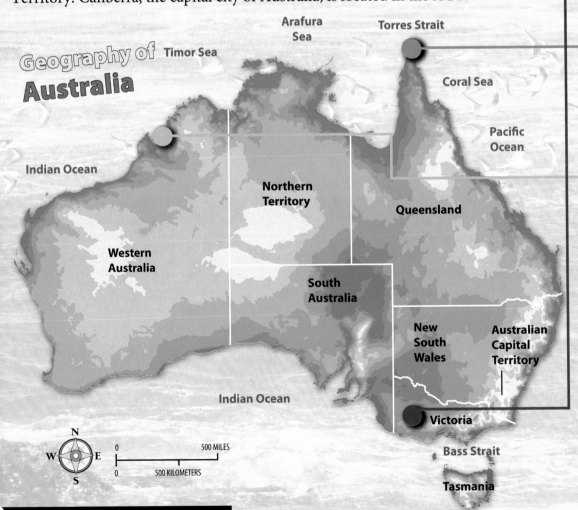

Geography of Australia

Arafura Sea

Timor Sea

Torres Strait

Coral Sea

Pacific Ocean

Indian Ocean

Northern Territory

Queensland

Western Australia

South Australia

New South Wales

Australian Capital Territory

Indian Ocean

Victoria

Bass Strait

Tasmania

N W E S

0 — 500 MILES
0 — 500 KILOMETERS

Grampians National Park, in Victoria, has many well-known landforms, including a canyon called the Grand Canyon. Grampians is a popular destination for bushwalking, which combines hiking and camping.

Cape York, in northern Queensland, is a remote peninsula, or area of land surrounded on three sides by water. The peninsula is home to a rare cloud formation called Morning Glory, which can stretch for thousands of miles (km) in early morning.

The only waterfalls on Earth where the water flows horizontally are in Western Australia at **Talbot Bay**. There, the tides force water through narrow passages in the cliffs.

LAND AND CLIMATE

Australia is the smallest of the seven continents, but mainland Australia is the world's largest island. The nation of Australia, which includes the mainland, Tasmania, and other islands, covers approximately 2.97 million square miles (7.69 million square kilometers). This is about four-fifths the size of the United States.

Australia is the lowest and flattest of the world's continents. All other continents have taller mountains. About 90 percent of Australian land features plains or plateaus. Plains are flat areas with few trees. Plateaus are areas of flat high ground. The continent's lowest point is a lakebed in South Australia, called Lake Eyre. It is about 50 feet (15 meters) below sea level. The lakebed receives little rain and is usually dry. Overall, about 20 percent of the continent is desert.

The mainland is divided into three land regions, called the Eastern Highlands, the Central Lowlands, and the Western Plateau. The Eastern Highlands receives the most rainfall of the three land regions. Found along the east coast, the Eastern Highlands has high plateaus, plains, and a chain of mountains called the Great Dividing Range. This chain extends north–south for 2,300 miles (3,700 km). The Great Dividing Range has Australia's highest mountain, Mount Kosciusko.

The slopes of the Great Dividing Range divide the drainage, or water flow, of the continent. To the east, rivers flow toward the Pacific. To the west, most rivers empty into the Indian Ocean. Waterways west of the Great Dividing Range include the Murray River, Australia's longest.

The Three Sisters is a rock formation in the Blue Mountains of New South Wales, part of the Eastern Highlands region.

Australia's Central Lowlands is a flat region in the middle of the mainland. In the Central Lowlands, the riverbeds remain dry, except during rare periods of heavy rainfall. Grass and shrubs cover much of the region. Other parts are desert.

The Western Plateau, sometimes called the Australian Shield, covers the continent's west. Much of this region is flat desert. However, there are also some low mountain ranges, as well as areas where grass and shrubs grow.

Most of Australia has warm summers and mild winters. The northern part of the continent is within the **tropics**. This region has warm or hot weather year-round. The tropical portion of Australia has a wet season from November to March, when most of the rainfall occurs.

The Murray River is **1,572 miles** (2,530 km) **long**.

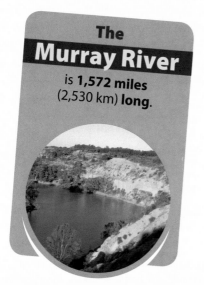

Mount Kosciusko stands **7,310 feet** (2,228 m) **tall**.

PLANTS AND ANIMALS

Kangaroos are the largest marsupials on Earth. They hop on their hind legs and use their strong tails for balance.

Australia has thousands of **species** of plants. The Wet Tropics is a rugged area in northeastern Queensland that has many rivers, waterfalls, and mountains. More than 3,000 plant species are found there. In central Australia, colorful wildflowers blanket the deserts after rare rainfalls. Milkmaids, orchids, and honeypots are some of the flowers that grow well in southern Australia.

Acacia trees and shrubs are found throughout the continent. Nearly 1,000 acacia species grow in Australia. Another common plant is the **eucalyptus** tree.

Australia's more than 140 marsupial species include kangaroos, koalas, and wombats. Bats and dingoes are among the native **mammals** that are not marsupials. Unlike most mammals, Australia's platypus and echidna are monotremes. This means they are mammals that lay eggs.

Australia's hundreds of bird species include the kookaburra and lyrebird. Many types of flightless birds live on the continent. One of these is the emu, the world's second-largest kind of bird, after the ostrich. More than 800 reptile species are found in Australia, including the tuatara, saltwater crocodile, and shingle-backed skink. The continent is home to a number of **venomous** snakes.

The wildflower blue leschenaultia is native to Western Australia and grows well in sandy or rocky soil.

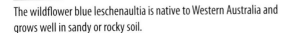

NATURAL RESOURCES

Land that supports agriculture is an important natural resource in Australia. About 10 percent of the continent's land is suitable for farming. Wheat, sugarcane, grapes, barley, cotton, and sunflowers are some of Australia's major crops. Sunflowers are used to produce sunflower oil.

About 60 percent of the continent's land can be used for ranching. Many ranchers raise sheep for their wool or cattle for their meat. Australia is the world's largest **exporter** of wool.

Australia's mineral resources include coal, copper, gold, iron ore, lead, nickel, silver, tin, zinc, tungsten, and bauxite, which contains aluminum. Australia is the world's leading bauxite producer. The continent also has deposits of natural gas and petroleum, or crude oil.

Mining was important to the development of the Australian continent by European settlers. Coal was discovered in the late 1700s. This allowed for the expansion of new settlements, since the coal could be used as fuel. In the 1800s, Australians began mining gold, lead, and copper, and these mining operations produced large profits.

Diamonds and other gemstones are mined in Australia. Queensland, New South Wales, and South Australia produce more than 95 percent of the world's opals. Australia has three main types, which are black, white, and boulder opals. Most of these gemstones are found in remote outback deserts. They are made of **silica** and water.

Australian sheep stations, or ranches, raise more than 70 million sheep.

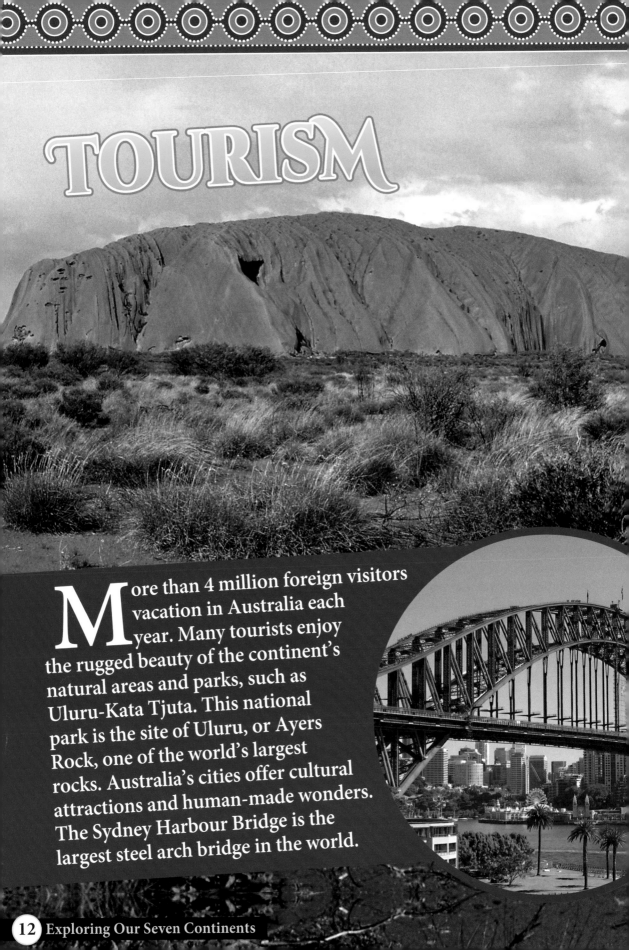

TOURISM

More than 4 million foreign visitors vacation in Australia each year. Many tourists enjoy the rugged beauty of the continent's natural areas and parks, such as Uluru-Kata Tjuta. This national park is the site of Uluru, or Ayers Rock, one of the world's largest rocks. Australia's cities offer cultural attractions and human-made wonders. The Sydney Harbour Bridge is the largest steel arch bridge in the world.

Attractions in Sydney, Australia's largest city, include the Sydney Opera House. Known for its **architecture**, the building features sail-shaped structures on its roof. Sydney, Melbourne, and other cities have museums, shopping districts, restaurants, and theaters.

Kangaroo Island, in South Australia, attracts visitors for its beaches in the Stokes Bay area on the north coast. On the west end of the island is Flinders Chase National Park. This is where the Remarkable Rocks are found, including rocks shaped like animals, castles, and huge teeth. On the east end of Kangaroo Island, visitors can camp, hike, and kayak in the Antechamber Bay area.

Tourists **SCUBA** dive through schools of fish and giant clams in the Great Barrier Reef. This underwater **ecosystem** extends for about 1,500 miles (2,400 km) along the coast. Much of the reef system is protected in Great Barrier Reef Marine Park. Visitors can sail around the reefs or snorkel in the clear surface waters.

Those interested in ancient history can view rock art created by Aboriginal Australians thousands of years ago. Uluru, a **sacred** place in Aboriginal culture, is in the Northern Territory. Aboriginal Australians prefer that visitors not climb Uluru, but the rock can be viewed on walking, camel, helicopter, or motorcycle tours.

Operas and concerts have been performed at the Sydney Opera House since 1973.

The Bungle Bungle Range in Western Australia's Purnululu National Park is another well-known attraction. Over millions of years, layers of rock and algae, which are small plants related to seaweed, formed mounds that look like beehives. Rock formations, pools of water, and palms surround these orange-and-black striped mounds.

Tasmania's natural areas include about 3.4 million acres (1.4 million hectares) of rain forest and alpine, or mountainous, land. Nearly half of Tasmania's land area is being protected from development. Visitors to Tasmania can hike in the Hartz Mountains or walk along the shoreline of Australia's deepest lake, Lake St. Clair.

The Remarkable Rocks were formed over a period of **500 million years**.

Skyrail, which moves above the treetops in a rain forest near Cairns, Queensland, is one of the **world's longest** gondola rides.

INDUSTRY

The country of Australia has a large economy, the measure of its wealth and resources. The Australian economy has been steadily expanding in recent years. The nation's **gross domestic product** (GDP) is more than $1.3 trillion. Only 11 other countries have GDPs that are larger than Australia's.

Manufacturing and other industries that produce goods account for almost 30 percent of Australia's GDP. About one-fifth of Australian workers have jobs in these industries. Many factories are located in and around the cities of Melbourne, Sydney, Brisbane, and Adelaide.

Products manufactured in Australia include industrial machinery, chemicals, ships, and other transportation equipment. The nation makes goods, such as explosives, that are needed by its mining industry. Mills in Australia use the country's iron ore to produce steel.

Some of Australia's factories process agricultural products into food items sold in stores. Wool from the country's sheep is used to manufacture fabrics and clothing. Most of the continent is not forested, but wood from Australia's forests is made into goods, such as furniture and paper.

Other important Australian industries include companies that are involved in telecommunications. These companies manufacture products such as mobile phones. They also provide internet access.

Refineries in Australia process crude oil into gasoline and other usable products.

GOODS AND SERVICES

More than three-fourths of Australian workers are employed in service jobs. These people provide services to others rather than produce goods. Service workers include bankers, teachers, doctors and nurses, bus drivers, hotel employees, restaurant workers, and tour guides. The tourism industry employs about 8 percent of Australian workers.

Trade with other countries is important to Australia's economy. Australia sells about $188 billion worth of goods yearly to other nations. Besides wool, leading Australian exports include iron ore, coal, gold, beef, and wheat. More than one-half of Australia's exports are bought by countries in eastern Asia. This includes almost one-third of all exports that are purchased by China.

Australia **imports** more than $200 billion worth of goods each year. Major imports include computers and office machines, telecommunications equipment, and refined petroleum products that are used in engines. The countries from which Australia buys the most imports include China, the United States, and Japan.

Australian farms produce about $4.5 billion worth of wheat that is exported yearly.

Iron ore accounts for **20%** of Australian exports.

More than **275,000** Australians work as **teachers**.

INDIGENOUS PEOPLES

Many **archaeologists** believe the first people to reach Australia traveled to the continent from Southeast Asia about 50,000 years ago. Over time, many different groups of Aboriginal Australians developed in various regions of the continent. They gathered plants and hunted animals for food. These early peoples invented the boomerang, a curved stick that, when thrown, returns to the thrower. It was used for hunting.

Traditional Aboriginal culture includes belief in the Dreaming, or Dreamtime, which is said to have begun long ago and to have no end. During the Dreaming, mythical beings created the natural world and all living things. They also created rules for people's behavior toward one another. Places where mythical beings performed important actions or were changed into natural objects are considered sacred sites.

Many Aboriginal Australians died in conflicts with European settlers, beginning in the late 1700s. Larger numbers died from diseases brought to Australia for the first time by Europeans. Aboriginal Australians were pushed off their traditional lands. Many were forced onto **reserves**.

More than 100,000 sites featuring rock art created by Aboriginal Australians have been discovered throughout Australia.

Aboriginal Australians mapped travel routes by passing along knowledge of landmarks, such as sharp turns in a river.

THE AGE OF EXPLORATION

European explorers reached the waters north of Australia in the 1500s. A Portuguese explorer was likely the first European to see New Guinea. This is a large island northeast of the Australian continent. Spanish explorers also reached New Guinea.

In 1606, Luis Vaez de Torres of Portugal sailed through the passage between New Guinea and Australia. This body of water was later named the Torres Strait. That same year, Dutch explorer Willem Jansz reached the northern coast of Australia. He believed that he had arrived at New Guinea.

After Captain Cook landed south of present-day Sydney in 1770, he named the body of water off the coast Botany Bay, because of the large variety of plants in the area.

The Dutch were the first Europeans to begin exploring the Australian continent. In 1616, Dutch sailor Dirk Hartog landed on an island in present-day Western Australia. In 1642, Dutch explorer Abel Tasman sailed around the Australian mainland. During this trip, he visited a nearby island. Tasman named it Van Diemen's Land, after Anthony van Diemen. He was the head of the Dutch East India Company, the company that paid for Tasman's voyage. In 1856, the island Tasman found was renamed Tasmania.

The British soon followed the Dutch. British sea captain James Cook sailed along the eastern coast of Australia in 1770. He claimed the area for Great Britain. Cook named the region New South Wales.

EARLY SETTLERS

British sea captain Arthur Phillip established the first permanent European settlement in Australia. Phillip set sail from Great Britain on May 13, 1787. He had 11 ships, known as the First Fleet. They carried more than 1,000 people. The ships arrived at Botany Bay on January 18, 1788.

Phillip and his ships had traveled 15,000 miles (24,000 km) to reach Australia. He spent a few days at Botany Bay. Then, he moved the First Fleet farther north, to a location he believed was better. On January 26, the ships arrived at a site the British named Port Jackson. Eventually, this settlement developed into the city of Sydney.

Most of the passengers in the First Fleet had been taken from British prisons. British officials planned to use Australia as a penal colony, or a place where convicts could be forced to relocate and work for the benefit of Great Britain. Conditions were difficult at first. Very few of the prisoners had experience with farming or construction. Their lack of farming skills, combined with the poor soil in the area, resulted in severe food shortages.

In the early 1790s, two more fleets transported prisoners to New South Wales. Convicts were also sent to other parts of the continent to create additional settlements. The first settlers who were not prisoners arrived in 1793.

The capital cities of Australia's states are all at the locations of early settlements. Hobart, Tasmania, was first settled in 1804. In 1824, a penal colony was established along the Brisbane River. This settlement became the city of Brisbane, the capital of Queensland. Captain James Stirling led a group of free settlers to build a colony along the Swan River in 1829. Located in Western Australia, this settlement became known as Perth. A settlement at Port Phillip Bay was established in 1835. Today, Port Phillip is known as Melbourne, the capital of Victoria. Adelaide, in South Australia, was settled in 1836. Sydney is the capital of the present-day state of New South Wales.

The old church at Tasmania's Port Arthur penal colony is now a museum and historic site.

By 1839, there were twice as many free settlers as there were convicts in Australia. The British government officially ended the policy of transporting prisoners there in 1868. Six separate British colonies developed on the continent during the 1800s. In 1901, the colonies united to form the independent country of Australia.

Each year on January 26, Australians celebrate their national holiday, called Australia Day. However, many Aboriginal Australians do not celebrate the holiday. Some call the date Invasion Day.

More than **12,500 convicts** lived at Port Arthur between **1830 and 1877**.

POPULATION

The population of Australia has grown a great deal since the first British settlers arrived. More than 24 million people live in the nation of Australia today. However, the **population density** in Australia is lower than in almost every other country. On average, there are only 3 people per 0.4 square miles (1 sq. km) of land in Australia.

The population is not divided evenly across the continent. About 90 percent of Australians live in urban areas, or cities and towns. This is double the percentage a century ago. The population is growing quickly in and around the capitals of Australia's states and territories. The fastest-growing area is the Molonglo Valley, near Canberra in the ACT. The number of people living in this area has more than doubled in recent years.

Almost 30 percent of Australians were born on a different continent. Another 20 percent of the population has at least one parent who was born outside Australia. After World War II, which ended in 1945, the Australian government welcomed European **immigrants** who were homeless due to the fighting. Many immigrants came from Eastern and Southern Europe. The number of immigrants from Asia and the Middle East started increasing in the 1970s.

Today, most Australians have European **ancestry**. People of Asian ancestry make up about 7 percent of the population. Aboriginal Australians account for 3 percent.

On Australia Day, people of many backgrounds celebrate with special events such as parades.

POLITICS AND GOVERNMENT

The Australian government was established by a **constitution** that went into effect in 1901, when the nation became independent. Australia is a **monarchy**. The queen or king of Great Britain is the head of state. She or he is represented in Australia by an appointed official called the governor-general. However, the governor-general has very little power over government decisions.

Australia is also a democracy. This is a type of government in which the people elect leaders to represent them. All Australians age 18 or older must vote in elections.

The country's laws are made by a parliament, or legislature. It consists of the House of Representatives and the Senate. Their members are elected. The leader of the political party that wins the most seats in the House of Representatives becomes the prime minister, or head of the government.

The prime minister selects other members of parliament to form his or her cabinet, or group of advisers. These people also lead different departments of the government. The prime minister and cabinet members often propose new laws and convince members of parliament to pass them.

The Australian government is a federal system. This means the national government makes major decisions regarding foreign affairs, trade with other nations, defense, immigration, and other policies affecting the whole country. Each state or territory has its own government, too. State and territorial governments are responsible for matters such as education and health care in their areas. The heads of state governments are called premiers.

Both the House of Representatives and the Senate meet in the building called Parliament House, in Canberra.

CULTURAL GROUPS

Australia is sometimes considered part of **Oceania**. In some ways, Australia's early culture developed like cultures on smaller islands in this region. Aboriginal Australians practiced their traditions for centuries without having any contact with other peoples. Later, British settlers had a major influence on Australian culture. This is symbolized in the Australian flag, which has the British flag in one corner.

Today, more Australians have British ancestry than any other cultural heritage. However, people have come to Australia from more than 150 countries around the world. Canberra celebrates its many cultural communities with a two-week Multicultural Festival. This annual citywide celebration has food, entertainment, and exhibits from around the world. Recent events included in the festival have had names such as Indigenous Showcase, African Showcase, Greek Glendi, India in the City, and Celtic Showcase.

Many cultural groups live in Sydney, including people of Greek, Italian, Vietnamese, Korean, and Chinese heritage. People from each culture live throughout the city, but some communities feature certain groups. For example, many people of Asian heritage live on the city's west side in Cabramatta, also known as Little Asia.

Australia's largest Asian festival takes place in Cabramatta to celebrate the Lunar New Year. There are fireworks displays, lion dancers, and parades. Year-round, shops and restaurants in Cabramatta's Freedom Plaza sell Asian products.

In Melbourne, the Italian community is one of the city's largest cultural groups. Beginning in the late 1800s, many people from Italy also settled in New South Wales. The New Italy Museum, in Woodburn, New South Wales, has historical exhibits that tell the story of Italian immigration.

British and other European settlers brought Christian faiths to Australia. Today, about 60 percent of Australians are Christians. The largest number of Christians follow a Protestant faith. About one-fourth of Australians are Roman Catholic. Other religions practiced by Australians include Buddhism, Hinduism, and Islam, the faith of Muslims.

English is the most common language spoken in Australia. Australian English is similar to British English, but it includes unique phrases and words. A special kind of English developed over time in Australia.

Almost one-fourth of Australians speak a language other than English at home. Languages commonly spoken include Mandarin, Italian, Arabic, Cantonese, Greek, Vietnamese, Spanish, Hindi, German, and Filipino or Tagalog. About 120 languages that developed among Aboriginal Australians are still in daily use.

The annual Color Run in Sydney is a running event inspired by the Hindu festival Holi, during which people throw colored powders on one another to celebrate the change from winter to spring.

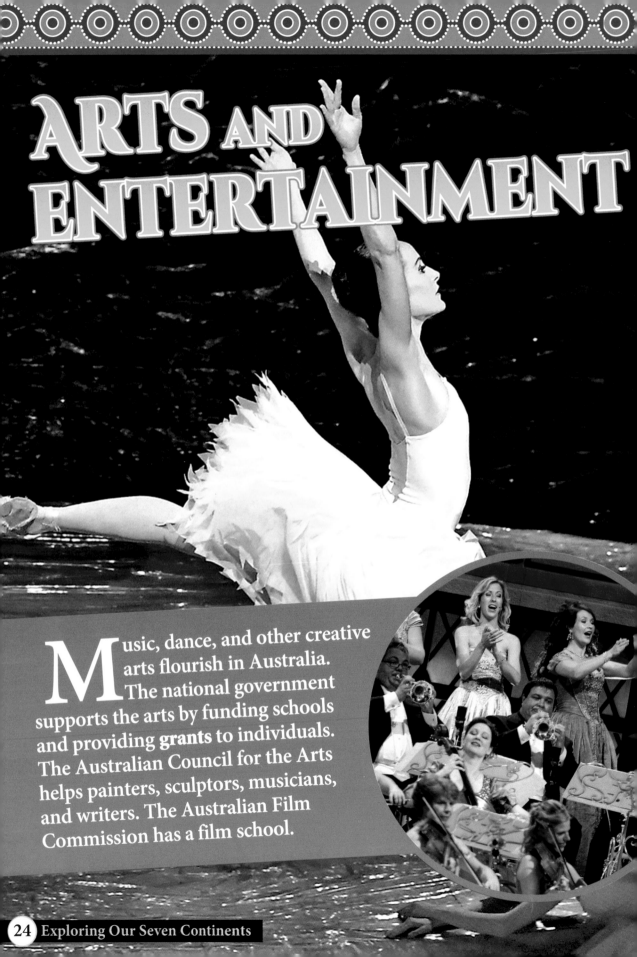

ARTS and ENTERTAINMENT

Music, dance, and other creative arts flourish in Australia. The national government supports the arts by funding schools and providing **grants** to individuals. The Australian Council for the Arts helps painters, sculptors, musicians, and writers. The Australian Film Commission has a film school.

Opera Australia is one of the continent's leading performing arts companies. This opera company performs each year at Arts Centre Melbourne and the Sydney Opera House. The company also stages performances elsewhere in Australia and around the world.

Other important arts companies include the Australian Ballet. With hundreds of shows each year, this dance company is one of the world's busiest. The Australian Ballet performs in cities and towns across Australia, as well as in other countries.

Symphony Services International assists with the development and presentation of music for orchestras. The group supports six symphonies. They are the Adelaide, Melbourne, Queensland, Sydney, Tasmanian, and West Australian Symphony Orchestras.

Australians also take pride in their visual and written arts. The National Gallery of Australia, in Canberra, houses thousands of artworks by Australian, Asian, and other artists. In 1973, fiction writer Patrick White won the Nobel Prize for Literature. He was the first Australian to win this award. His best-known books include *The Tree of Man*, *Voss*, and *Riders in the Chariot*. In 1964, Oodgeroo Noonuccal was the first Aboriginal Australian to publish a book of poetry. It is titled *We Are Going*. Noonuccal was an actor and artist, as well as a poet, and she worked for Aboriginal rights.

Actors Hugh Jackman and Nicole Kidman appeared together in the movie *Australia*, which they introduced at Sydney's Museum of Contemporary Art in 2008.

Many well-known film actors come from Australia. Born in Hawai'i, Nicole Kidman moved to her parents' hometown of Sydney when young. Before going to Hollywood and appearing in 1989's *Dead Calm*, Kidman starred in Australian film and television productions. At age 16, she won her first movie role, in *Bush Christmas*. This film is a holiday classic in Australia.

Actor Naomi Watts was born in Great Britain but raised in Australia. Hugh Jackman, known for his role as Wolverine in the X-Men movies, is from Sydney. Chris Hemsworth was born in Melbourne. He is known, in part, for his role as Thor in the Marvel Universe films.

Museums in Australia have more than **2.8 million** works of art.

Ticket sales for **Chris Hemsworth's** first two **Thor** movies totaled more than **$1 billion.**

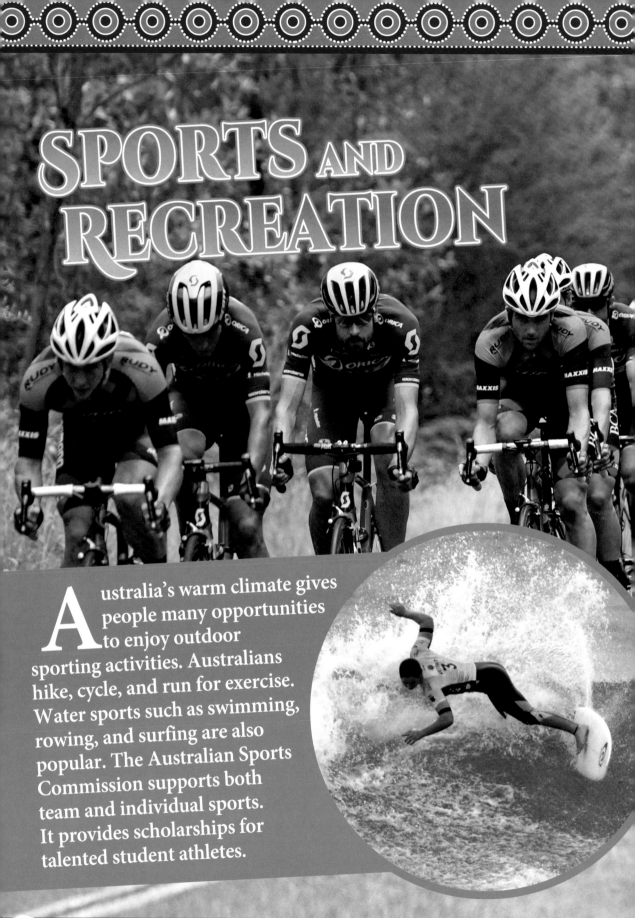

SPORTS AND RECREATION

Australia's warm climate gives people many opportunities to enjoy outdoor sporting activities. Australians hike, cycle, and run for exercise. Water sports such as swimming, rowing, and surfing are also popular. The Australian Sports Commission supports both team and individual sports. It provides scholarships for talented student athletes.

Many Australian cities have professional sports teams, and national teams represent Australia in international competitions. Cricket is a popular sport played on an oval field with two teams of 11 players. Players use a bat that is round on one side and flat on the other to hit a ball slightly larger than a baseball. Games can take several days to play. The Australian national team competes against cricket teams from around the world.

Australian rules football, rugby league, and rugby union are three other team sports with many followers. Teams try to score points by pushing past an opposing team toward a goal at the end of the playing field. Many women's teams compete in netball, which is played on a court and is similar to basketball. Instead of a basket, there is a goal with a hoop at each end of the court. Players pass the ball, which cannot touch the ground.

Australian athletes have had success at the Olympic Games. Runner Cathy Freeman is a well-known Australian athlete. In 1992, she was the first Aboriginal Australian to represent Australia at the Olympic Games, which were held that year in Barcelona, Spain. Four years later, Freeman won the silver medal in the 400-meter race at the 1996 Summer Olympics in Atlanta, Georgia. At the 2000 Summer Games, held in Sydney, she won the gold medal in the 400-meter event.

In the Big Bash League, cricket teams from Australia's largest cities compete against one another.

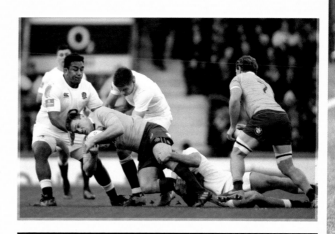

Australia's national rugby team, nicknamed the Wallabies, competes against teams from other areas, such as England.

Cathy Freeman's gold-medal win was Australia's **100th Olympic gold medal**.

Mapping Australia

We use many tools to interpret maps and to understand the locations of features such as cities, states, lakes, and rivers. The map below has many tools to help interpret information on the map of Australia.

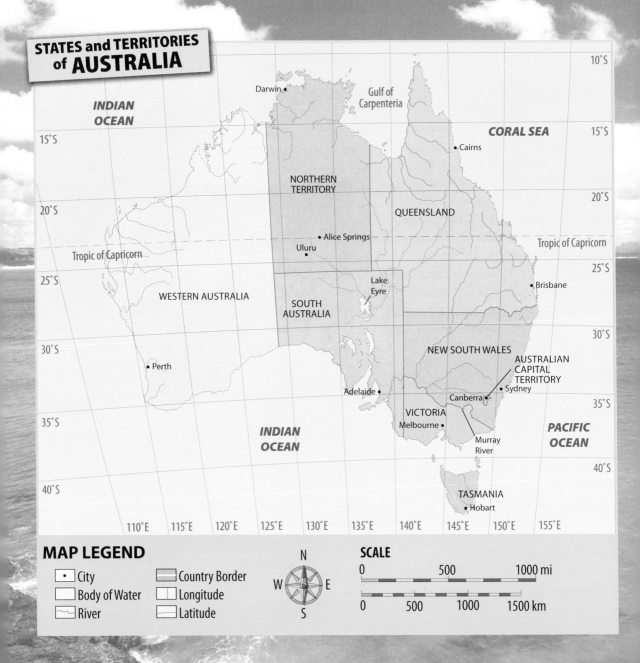

STATES and TERRITORIES of AUSTRALIA

INDIAN OCEAN

10°S

Darwin

Gulf of Carpenteria

CORAL SEA

15°S

15°S

Cairns

NORTHERN TERRITORY

20°S

20°S

QUEENSLAND

Alice Springs

Tropic of Capricorn

Uluru

Tropic of Capricorn

25°S

25°S

Lake Eyre

Brisbane

WESTERN AUSTRALIA

SOUTH AUSTRALIA

30°S

30°S

NEW SOUTH WALES

Perth

AUSTRALIAN CAPITAL TERRITORY

Adelaide

Sydney

Canberra

35°S

35°S

VICTORIA

INDIAN OCEAN

Melbourne

PACIFIC OCEAN

Murray River

40°S

40°S

40°S

TASMANIA

Hobart

110°E 115°E 120°E 125°E 130°E 135°E 140°E 145°E 150°E 155°E

MAP LEGEND

- City
- Body of Water
- River
- Country Border
- Longitude
- Latitude

N
W   E
S

SCALE

0   500   1000 mi

0   500   1000   1500 km

Mapping Tools

- The compass rose shows north, south, east, and west. The points in between represent northeast, northwest, southeast, and southwest.

- The map scale shows that the distances on a map represent much longer distances in real life. If you measure the distance between objects on a map, you can use the map scale to calculate the actual distance in miles or kilometers between those two points.

- The lines of latitude and longitude are long lines that appear on maps. The lines of latitude run east to west and measure how far north or south of the equator a place is located. The lines of longitude run north to south and measure how far east or west of the Prime Meridian a place is located. A location on a map can be found by using the two numbers where latitude and longitude meet. This number is called a coordinate and is written using degrees and direction. For example, the city of Adelaide would be found at 35°S and 139°E on a map.

Using the map and the appropriate tools, complete the activities below.

Locating with latitude and longitude
1. Which Australian state is found at 30°S and 125°E?
2. What body of water is found at 15°S and 140°E?
3. Which Australian city is found on the map using the coordinates 38°S and 145°E?

Distances between points
4. Using the map scale and a ruler, calculate the approximate distance between the cities of Perth and Sydney.
5. Using the map scale and a ruler, find the approximate distance between Melbourne and Hobart.
6. Use the map scale to figure out what landmark is found about 150 miles (240 km) southwest of Alice Springs.

Map it yourself
7. Using latitude and longitude lines as a guide, write out coordinates that would meet at any point along the Murray River.
8. Find any two places on the map. Figure out the actual distance between them, using the map scale.

Quiz Time

Test your knowledge of Australia by answering these questions.

1 What is the approximate length of the Great Barrier Reef?

2 About what percentage of Australia's land is suitable for farming?

3 Australia produces 95 percent of the world's supply of which gemstone?

4 Who were the first people to live in Australia?

5 What is Australia's lowest point?

6 What is the capital city of Australia?

7 Which city developed on the site of the Port Jackson settlement?

8 Which Australian sport is much like basketball?

9 In what year did Australia become independent from Great Britain?

10 Who was the first Australian to win the Nobel Prize for Literature?

ANSWERS 1. 1,500 miles (2,400 km) 2. 10 percent 3. Opal 4. Aboriginal Australians 5. Lake Eyre 6. Canberra 7. Sydney 8. Netball 9. 1901 10. Patrick White

Key Words

ancestry: people in the past from whom a culture or a person has descended

archaeologists: scientists who study objects and remains from the past to learn about ancient cultures

architecture: the style in which buildings are designed

constitution: a written document stating a government's basic principles and laws

corals: tiny sea animals with hard skeletons that live in large groups and form structures called reefs in warm coastal waters

ecosystem: plants and animals that are living together in an environment and need one another for survival

equator: an imaginary circle around Earth that separates the Northern and Southern Hemispheres, or halves, of the planet

eucalyptus: a tall evergreen tree native to Australia, with a strong-smelling oil in its leaves

exporter: a seller of goods to other countries or areas

grants: gifts of money usually provided for a specific purpose or to support a certain type of activity

gross domestic product: the total value of goods produced and services provided yearly in a country or an area

immigrants: people who move to a different country to live

imports: buys from other countries

mammals: animals that have hair or fur and feed mother's milk to their young

marsupials: animals that carry their young in a pouch on the mother's stomach

monarchy: a type of government headed by a queen, a king, or another member of a royal family who inherits his or her leadership position

Oceania: a large region in the central and southern Pacific Ocean with many islands

population density: the number of people living per unit of area

reserves: areas of land set aside for Aboriginal Australians

sacred: thought to be holy or worthy of worship

SCUBA: an abbreviation for Self-Contained Underwater Breathing Apparatus, a device that includes a container of air and that is used by divers to breathe underwater

silica: a chemical that makes up the major part of most types of sand

species: groups of individuals with common characteristics

tropics: the area of Earth that is closest to the equator and that lies between two imaginary lines known as the Tropic of Cancer and the Tropic of Capricorn

venomous: referring to animals that inject venom, a poisonous substance, into their victims when they bite them

Index

Log on to www.av2books.com

AV² by Weigl brings you media enhanced books that support active learning. Go to www.av2books.com, and enter the special code found on page 2 of this book. You will gain access to enriched and enhanced content that supplements and complements this book. Content includes video, audio, weblinks, quizzes, a slide show, and activities.

AV² Online Navigation

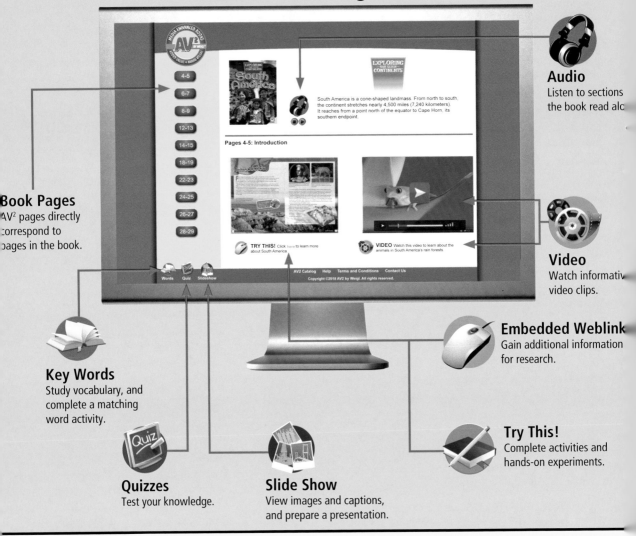

Audio
Listen to sections the book read alo

Book Pages
AV² pages directly correspond to pages in the book.

Video
Watch informativ video clips.

Key Words
Study vocabulary, and complete a matching word activity.

Embedded Weblink
Gain additional information for research.

Quizzes
Test your knowledge.

Slide Show
View images and captions, and prepare a presentation.

Try This!
Complete activities and hands-on experiments.

AV² was built to bridge the gap between print and digital. We encourage you to tell us what you like and what you want to see in the future.

Sign up to be an AV² Ambassador at www.av2books.com/ambassador.

Due to the dynamic nature of the Internet, some of the URLs and activities provided as part of AV² by Weigl may have changed or ceased to exist. AV² by Weigl accepts no responsibility for any such changes. All media enhanced books are regularly monitored to update addresses and sites in a timely manner. Contact AV² by Weigl at 1-866-649-3445 or av2books@weigl.com with any questions, comments, or feedback.